WEEKLY WR READER®
EARLY LEARNING LIBRARY

STORMS
DUST STORMS

by Jim Mezzanotte
Reading consultant: Susan Nations, M.Ed.,
author/literacy coach/consultant in literacy development
Science and curriculum consultant: Debra Voege, M.A.,
science and math curriculum resource teacher

Please visit our web site at: garethstevens.com
For a free color catalog describing Weekly Reader® Early Learning Library's list
of high-quality books, call 1-877-445-5824 (USA) or 1-800-387-3178 (Canada).
Weekly Reader® Early Learning Library's fax: (414) 336-0164.

Library of Congress Cataloging-in-Publication Data

Mezzanotte, Jim.
    Dust storms / by Jim Mezzanotte.
      p. cm. — (Storms)
    Includes bibliographical references and index.
    ISBN-13: 978-0-8368-7911-7 (lib. bdg.)
    ISBN-13: 978-0-8368-7918-6 (softcover)
    1. Dust storms—Juvenile literature. I. Title.
  QC958.M49   2007
  551.55'9—dc22   2006033919

This edition first published in 2007 by
Weekly Reader® Early Learning Library
A Member of the WRC Media Family of Companies
330 West Olive Street, Suite 100
Milwaukee, WI 53212 USA

Editorial direction: Mark Sachner
Editor: Barbara Kiely Miller
Art direction, cover and layout design: Tammy West
Photo research: Diane Laska-Swanke

Photo credits: Cover, title, pp. 5, 7, 12, 13, 15, 16, 17, 19 © AP Images; p. 6 © Dr. Marli Miller/
Visuals Unlimited; p. 8 © Jane Thomas/Visuals Unlimited; p. 9 Kami Strunsee/© Weekly Reader
Early Learning Library; p. 11 Scott M. Krall/© Weekly Reader Early Learning Library; p. 18 NOAA;
p. 21 © Paul Stepan/Photo Researchers, Inc.

Printed in the United States of America

1 2 3 4 5 6 7 8 9 10 10 09 08 07 06

Table of Contents

Cover and title page: A wall of dust moves through Casa Grande, Arizona. The dust storm was so thick that people could not see anything.

CHAPTER 1

Here Comes a Dust Storm!

Have you ever watched a storm? The sky turns dark. Rain or snow begins to fall. But what if dust fell instead?

In a dust storm, strong winds blow big clouds of dust. The winds blow across the ground. They lift up sand or tiny pieces of rock and dirt.

A dust cloud can be thousands of feet tall. It moves quickly across the ground. It fills the air and blocks out the sunlight. People can only see things that are very close.

A large dust storm rolls over Phoenix, Arizona. The storm's strong winds kept planes from taking off and landing.

This sandy desert in California is called Death Valley. It is the hottest and driest place in North America.

Dust storms mostly happen in **arid** places. These are places that receive little rain. The ground is very dry there. The wind can easily blow away the soil.

Deserts are dry places. They get less than 10 inches (25 centimeters) of rain a year. Some deserts receive almost no rain. The ground is often sandy. Wind blows the sand, creating dust storms.

Sometimes, dust storms develop after a **drought**. For a long time, no rain falls. The ground turns dry and plants die. Sometimes, cattle or other livestock eat all the plants. The ground is uncovered and can blow away.

A dust storm may also appear above a lake bed, which is the bottom of a lake. The lake may dry up. With all the water gone, the lake bed becomes dry and dusty.

A farmer in China walks through a field of dying plants. Droughts in China have hurt the soil, people, and animals.

The Sahara Desert gets many dust storms. It is in northern Africa. The Sahara Desert is like a big sea of sand. It is about the same size as the United States!

Sand and dust blow across the Sahara Desert, the largest desert in the world.

This map shows the world's largest deserts. Clouds of dust from some deserts blow across the ocean to other countries.

Countries in the Middle East get dust storms. So does China. Australia gets them, too. The United States gets a few dust storms. States in the Southwest, such as Arizona and New Mexico, get the most storms.

CHAPTER 2

Dust Storms in Action

How do dust storms start? Heat can cause them.
The Sun warms air that is near the ground. The
warm air rises. This rising air creates winds that
lift up the dust.

A thunderstorm can bring a dust storm. This kind of dust storm is called a **haboob**. It forms in deserts.

Thunderclouds move over the desert. Cold winds blow down from the clouds and across the ground. The winds lift up the sand. At the front edge of the thunderstorm, a haboob forms.

cold winds

A dust storm may begin with a thundercloud's cold winds (*blue arrows*). They kick up a wall of dust and push the storm forward.

cold winds

dust storm

This dust storm in China turns daytime into night. Drivers keep their car lights on to see better in the storm.

A dust storm may last a few hours or a few days. No matter how long it lasts, it puts a lot of dust into the air.

Some dust falls back to the ground. Some stays in the air. This dust can travel hundreds of miles to other places.

Sand from Africa may end up in Europe, or it may travel even farther. It may end up on an island in the Caribbean Sea. Dust from China is blown across the ocean to the United States.

Sometimes, the dust in the air is mixed with raindrops. Then "mud rain" falls. The raindrops are like tiny drops of mud!

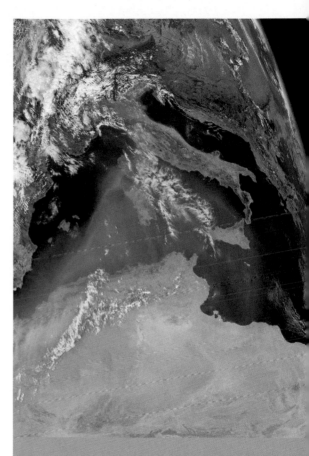

Sand from the Sahara Desert blows toward Europe in this photo taken from space. The dust (*light brown*) can be seen over the water.

CHAPTER 3

Dust Problems

A dust storm can be powerful. In the desert, it moves and reshapes big sand **dunes**. The storm can look like a huge wall of dust. A dust storm can cause many problems.

The dust flies everywhere. It gets inside houses, even if all the doors and windows are closed. The dust gets into machines and causes them to break down.

If you are outside, the blowing dust stings your skin. It gets inside your clothing. It blows into your eyes, nose, and mouth, too. People have trouble breathing in a dust storm. They have to cover their faces.

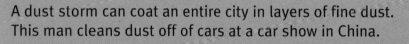

A dust storm can coat an entire city in layers of fine dust. This man cleans dust off of cars at a car show in China.

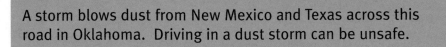

A storm blows dust from New Mexico and Texas across this road in Oklahoma. Driving in a dust storm can be unsafe.

When a dust storm hits, the dust buries roads. People cannot see where to go. Airports and schools may have to close.

Dust storms can be bad for farmers. Dust lands on **crops** and kills them. The strong winds take away the **topsoil**, the dirt on the surface of the ground. Plants need good, rich topsoil to grow.

Farmers plant trees on a hillside in China. Trees block the wind and help stop the soil from blowing away or becoming a desert.

A mountain of dust heads toward a Texas town in April 1935. One of the Dust Bowl's worst storms took place that month.

In the 1930s, dust storms hit many U.S. farms. They struck farms in the middle of the country. This area became known as the **Dust Bowl**.

A drought turned the ground dry. Then, winds took away the topsoil, creating dust storms. Farmers in the Dust Bowl could not grow crops.

A dust storm can cause health problems. People develop bad coughs when they breathe the dust. They may choke on it. The dust can carry diseases, too.

Cars and factories in cities can create smoke and other **pollution**. These substances rise into the air. When a dust storm comes, the pollution in the air mixes with the dust. It may be carried far away, landing in other places.

People who live with dust storms must cover their faces. This woman puts a mask on her dog to protect it from the dust, too.

CHAPTER 4

Living with Dust Storms

Scientists study dust storms. They use **satellites** that take pictures of the storms. They try to decide where the storms are heading. Then, they can warn people!

During a dust storm, scientists use an **anemometer** (an-uh-MOM-hu-tur) to know how fast the wind is blowing. This tool is a pole with cups on it. The cups spin around in the wind and measure its speed.

For some people, dust storms are part of life. They may live near deserts. They try to protect themselves when a storm comes.

These people wear special clothing. It covers their heads and bodies. They may wear **goggles** to keep the dust out of their eyes. When a dust storm is coming, they know how to stay safe.

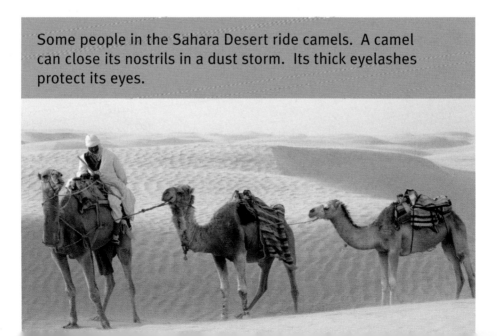

Some people in the Sahara Desert ride camels. A camel can close its nostrils in a dust storm. Its thick eyelashes protect its eyes.

Glossary

arid — getting very little rain, so the ground is dry and few plants can grow

crops — plants that farmers grow for food

drought — a time when little or no rain falls

dunes — hills made of sand

Dust Bowl — an area in the center of the United States where bad dust storms hit in the 1930s. The storms blew away the topsoil, so many farmers could no longer grow crops.

goggles — glasses that protect the eyes and fit snugly against the face

pollution — waste created by people that is harmful to living things

satellites — machines that orbit, or circle, Earth. They can send back pictures and information about what is happening on Earth.

topsoil — a layer of dirt on the surface of the ground that is good for growing crops

For More Information

Books

Droughts. Weather Update (series). Nathan Olson (Capstone)

Dust Bowl! The 1930s Black Blizzards. X-treme Disasters That Changed America (series). Richard H. Levey (Bearport Publishing)

Life in the Dust Bowl. Picture the Past (series). Sally Senzell Isaacs (Heinemann)

Weather. DK Eyewitness Guides (series). Brian Cosgrove (Penguin Books)

Web Site

Dust Storms and Their Damage
www.weru.ksu.edu/pics/dust_storms
See photos taken during and after dust storms.

Publisher's note to educators and parents: Our editors have carefully reviewed this Web site to ensure that it is suitable for children. Many Web sites change frequently, however, and we cannot guarantee that a site's future contents will continue to meet our high standards of quality and educational value. Be advised that children should be closely supervised whenever they access the Internet.

Index

About the Author

Jim Mezzanotte has written many books for children. He lives in Milwaukee, Wisconsin, with his wife and two sons. He has always been interested in the weather, especially big storms.